You'll Never Be Anyone Else

You'll Never Be Anyone Else

by
Rachael Clyne

Seren is the book imprint of
Poetry Wales Press Ltd.
Suite 6, 4 Derwen Road, Bridgend, Wales, CF31 1LH
www.serenbooks.com
facebook.com/SerenBooks
twitter@SerenBooks

The right of Rachael Clyne to be identified as
the author of this work has been asserted in accordance
with the Copyright, Designs and Patents Act, 1988.

© Rachael Clyne, 2023

ISBN: 978-1-78172-703-4
Ebook: 978-1-78172-704-1

A CIP record for this title is available from the British Library.

The publisher acknowledges the financial assistance of the Books Council of Wales.

Cover painting: 'The Session' by Carole Windham

Contents

Girl Golem	7
Sweety Pie	8
Three Piece Suite	9
Bedtime	10
Our Usual Walk	11
Tradition	12
Jew-a-lingo –	13
White/Other?	14
The SCHNOZZ	15
In Odesa's Moldovanko District	16
Leaving Odesa	17
Mr Shopping Trolley	18
Siblings	19
What can we talk about…	20
I cradle my grief	21
Girl Golem finds a foster home	22
True Romance – Comics for Girls	23
Waiting for Bread	24
My fifteen-year-old hymen	25
Proposal	26
Diva	27
Ronnie Scott's 1976	28
Susan Expects to Be Admired	29
Dateroo	30
A Man Threw Knives at Me	31
Girl Golem is Stranded in Marriage	32
Removing Her Face	33
Full Sail	34
Indoor Sport	35
Take the Medicine	36
Her Mind is Snagged	37
Girl Golem Wonders What to Wear	38
My Life as a Soap	39
Puzzled	40
Out of My Head	41
And Eat It	42
I Sketch Her as a Bird-headed Goddess	43
La Cuisine de L'Amour	44
Unfitting	45

Birls and Goys Come Out to Play   46
Power Cut   47
Girl Golem Looks Back   48
Tripp Reviews My Past   49
Dear Unborns   50
Be Grateful For Those Love Lessons   51
Tending the Wounded   52
Liberating the Senses   53
Seen   54
Because of Wet Grass   55
What I Asked of Life   56
Rewilding the Body   57
Sometime in the next ten years   58
You'll never be anyone else   59
Acknowledgements   60

Girl Golem

The night they blew life into her, she clung
bat-like to the womb-wall. A girl golem,
a late bonus, before the final egg dropped.
She divided, multiplied, her hand-buds bloomed;
her tail vanished into its coccyx and the lub-dub
of her existence was bigger than her nascent head.

She was made as a keep-watch,
in case new nasties tried to take them away.
The family called her *tchotchkele*, their little *cnadle*,
said she helped to make up for lost numbers –
as if she could compensate for millions.

With x-ray eyes, she saw she was trapped
in a home for the deaf and blind, watched them
blunder into each other's neuroses. Her task,
to hold up their world, be their assimilation ticket,
find a nice boy and *mazel tov* – grandchildren!

But she was a hotchpotch golem, a *schmutter* garment
that would never fit, trying to find answers
without a handbook. When she turned eighteen,
she walked away, went in search of her own kind,
tore their god from her mouth.

Golem: man made from clay and Kabbalistic spells, by rabbis to protect Jews from
persecution. Truth: אמת was written on his forehead and God's name on his tongue.
Tchotchkele (diminutive of tchotchke): a trinket, a cute child. *Mazel tov:* good luck.
Cnadle: a dumpling. *Schmutter:* a rag.

Sweety Pie

We always wanted a girl,
but you weren't the kiss-curl kind.
Grubby-kneed, nosepicker.
You tore the frocks grandma made.
You answered back. *How rude.*
You dimpled nicely though, when pressed
with a finger and grandma had big teeth.
She kept them in her pocket.
We told her to slip them in,
as you popped the oven on –
just a teeny shove.

Three Piece Suite

Mother, the rickety chair, teeters;
needs a wedge to steady her.
A chair from the Old Country,
carried on backs, luggage racks, smuggled

across borders. Father, a wooden
ironing board, hides in the under-stairs
cupboard, lost in the hiss of his steam-iron,
whistle of hearing aids and bash of his *klomper*.

Grandma, the leathery pouffe, smells
of olives, lemon tea and shit on shaky fingers.
Between chair, ironing board and pouffe,
I, their tailor's cushion, bristle with pins.

Klomper: a wooden block tailors used to bash out creases, when pressing garments.

Bedtime

The man behind the wardrobe gloops like hot Marmite. I try to ignore him then say in my loudest voice MY DADDY'S A POLICEMAN AND HE'S IN THE NEXT ROOM except he's not and he's deaf. Branch-fingers scratch to get in and the chimney moans. I know when it's the really-dark because I can't hear the TV anymore and there's only me. Just when I'm almost asleep the wall behind my head starts yelling, YOU BULLY…DON'T YOU YELL AT ME…BASTARD! I put my fingers in my ears till I'm falling asleep… then wall starts up again.

I tight squeeze my eyes for my friends Toad, Ratty and Tigger to rescue me. We get into Toad's Chitty Bang car and fly off through the sky which is soft and quiet. We loop-de-loop the happy-face moon. We play catch-stars and splash glitter all over the really-dark chanting, *POOP POOP!* until the shouting's stopped and I go to sleep.

Our Usual Walk

She gets it from me–

my smile, says mum.
My nose, says dad.

I'm the actress, says mum.
Well, I'm the artist, says dad.

Daughter-in-the-middle tries
to elbow them apart.

Dad says, *I have to be close,*
I can't help being deaf.

Mum-with-her-short-legs says,
I can't keep up.

Daughter tightens her lips,
her eyes fixed ahead.

Tradition

The *Mohel* wraps the tiny penis,
gives a finger of wine for baby to suck.

A dentist by trade, this is his special calling
removing foreskins with a v shaped blade

satisfying God's strange need
for all those bits of skin.

With new grandchild on his knee,
father turns ashen.

The women stand behind a curtain,
or in the kitchen, wait to catch falling men.

Mohel: a man who performs circumcision

Jew–a–lingo –
Code-switching for Jews– 1970 edition

Lesson 1 – *At Home*
- Emphasise emotions with vivid gestures.
- Always answer a question with a question.
- Angst is compulsory, as is *qvetch* and guilt.
- Joke in the old tongue. Smack lips round *schlep, lobbes, schlemozzle.*

Lesson 2 – *At Mealtime*
- It is usual to talk over each other with your mouth full.
- Expect more than you can eat.
- Learn to tolerate cold, chopped and boiled, gefilte fish – it's tradition.
- Compare Mother's strudel with Mrs Lipman's.
- When guests are present, grill them with personal questions.

Lesson 3 – *Away From Home*
- Avoid loud colours and remarks.
- Avoid complaining or personal feelings
- Avoid acting like a *nebech-dicker* victim.
- Avoid acting like a banker's wallet or a vegan-leftie.
- Yes both. You think I invent these *meshuggah* slurs?

Lesson 4 – *In Social Situations*
- When refused membership to local societies e.g. the golf club, apologise.
- If they call you *Jew girl* or ask what you do for Christmas, smile.
- Choose only words that are Formica-smooth.
- Never make a drama out of a trifle.
- Never dominate the conversation.
- Try not to interrupt. Try harder.
- Beware, those colour-coded smiles conceal teeth.

Qvetch: complain. *Schlep:* drag, haul. *Shmendrik:* a fool. *Lobbes:* a good for nothing (Polish). *Schlemozzlel:* a row. *Nebech-dicker:* pathetic person. *Meshuggah:* crazy.

White/Other?

What are you doing for Christmas?
I'm Jewish, I'd reply. *Yes,* they'd insist,
but what are you doing for Christmas?

Sheila said, *But that's just ignorance,*
not prejudice. Shamed for exaggerating,
as if ignorance has less sting.

It wasn't just the boy spitting *Christkiller,*
in my face or silent stare of classmates
when my best friend said,

You can't let Jews in. They'll only take over.
It was the tiny corrosion of men
whispering in my ear, *You Jewesses,*

so dark, exotic and people's low hiss,
You're so full on, such a victim.

At least with my skin
I can hide, be traitor to myself.

The SCHNOZZ

No cute buttons for us
No retroussé
just a big fuck-off hook
with wind tunnel nostrils
sucking up everyone's money
and stuffed with your Zio conspiracy bogies

Our NOSE grows
with the lies you tell about us
A *ganser macher* of *SCHNOZZELS*
a Geiger counter that detects
the whiff of the *Yid*
the reek of hatred

We walk into a room NOSE first
sniff out muttered asides
the glances that clock
our naked greedy
in-your-face
dodgy SCHNOZZ

Schnozzel: nose. *Ganser macher*: an important influencer.

15

In Odesa's Moldovanko District

Yiddish echoes through a mishmash
of courtyard tenements. Balconies strung
with washing, squawking kids. Cheek-by-jowl
neighbours chop vegetables into enamel bowls.
Between drug dealers and satellite dishes,
ghosts gather. Water sellers, tailors
and a shiver that runs up my back.

I hear Bubbe Sarah, who like Chagall's bride,
clutches her bouquet, floats over cobbles,
etched with trolleybus rails. Footfall
clanks on iron stairs, peeling walls
shouldered past, greased by hands.
A century of decay, but the chicken soup
spirit lingers. She whispers: This is where we lived.

Leaving Odesa

Under Tsarist law, if someone died in prison, the next of kin had to complete the sentence.

I wait for the Moscow train, knowing that under my feet
was once the debtor's prison where Grandma Sonia

was born and learned early how to finish a sentence –
the one her father left her. He died before his term was up.

The old Soviet terminus has plaques to men with sledgehammers.
I queue for the loo, a woman hands me correct rations of paper.

On the long green train, a steward in perky blue uniform
brings glasses of tea. I settle into linen sheets, watch TV soaps.

Through the window, I see grandma leaving this land,
a baby in her arms, her husband in his fine astrakhan hat.

This is how migrant tales become holiday destinations,
how debts are paid and how her roof became my ground.

Mr Shopping Trolley

Stuffed with newspapers
lifted from transport seats and bins,
dad was a shopping trolley.

His tailor's fingers itched
for snip of shears
and papercut swish.

Earpiece strapped to TV, sealed
in his deafness bubble, until we
blocked his view and waved in his face.

His control suite was stocked with
paper, scissors, biros, paperclips,
bulldog clips and Sellotape dispenser.

He sliced, spliced, stapled
and bunched his evenings
with random clippings.

Health risks of eating fungi.
The Odd History of Putney Sewers.
Cure for Arthritis Found.

Each point circled, crossed,
in red, black and/or blue. Sellotape
was his glue of choice. He applied it

to the base of kitchen units
and attaching batons across doorways,
as a DIY cockroach deterrent.

Instead of cheques to help with my bills,
he posted paper love-tokens: *Somerset's*
Last Coalmine, The Power of Vitamin K.

My inheritance – a pile
of twelve stuffed bags,
thrown out for refuse collection.

Siblings

You were always the five-year plan to my next giro.
The Putney to my Clapham Junction.
The Harrods to my Arding & Hobbs.

Yours, the fridge I binged from.
Your children, my sibling rivals.
Your husband, the lawyer to my marital folly.

Then I became the living to your dying.
The diamond Harrods didn't stock.
The cradle for your shrinking body.

I, the lullaby to your nightmare.
I, the older to your wiser.
I, the left behind to your gone-before.

What can we talk about...

when events in the rest
of the house no longer hold
meaning, when tomorrow
is a singular possibility

and the world outside
or any future stops
at your bedroom door?

I stutter, *my bus was late...*
but each word I utter
points to your departure.

Tending your body,
bathing together in silence –

the only conversation left.

I cradle my grief

sing it lullabies
keen with it
roar with it
hide it write it
speak it shout it
It keeps coming
back in waves
each time rising
each time deeper
until   I   wail
for   each   leafless   branch
each   leech   each   death
each   beech   each   dearth

each   drought   each   birth

each   beached   whale

until   it   contains   the   whole   world

Will   you   hold   it   for   me
Just   for   a   few   moments
Take care to support its head
DO NOT
let it
drop

Girl Golem finds a foster home

where *other* is a selling point.
Frightfully nice and *y'aright chuck*
side by side with posh, poor, fat, lean-
a ragamuffin motley of allsorts.
She was a trouper, a luvvie
slipping on cozzies and voices.

Normals have proper jobs, but we have the biz,
the stage-struck razz. We have
the hi-diddly-dee in our starry eyes.
An audience to cheer, a mask to wear,
a make'em laugh, make'em cry mask.

Those moments of Icarus high.
The electric jolt of her and an audience,
plugged in and soaring to *Neverland*.
In less than a breath –
all of us heavenly bodies.

Icarus and Golem fell back to Earth,
to the dole queue and an empty flat
craving the next fix of being paid
to be someone – anyone. There she sat,
smoking dog-ends of herself.

True Romance — Comics for Girls

We collided in the doorway of that smart café on the Strand:
    and/or at a tedious department meeting
    and/or on Waterloo bridge at dawn
    and/or by a lamppost, one foggy night.

I spilled coffee down my dress, mesmerised by
his velvet brown:
    and/or sparkling blue eyes, It was raining:
    and/or I was sunburnt.
We laughed. He gave me his hankie.
I wore my tartiest scarlet heels:
    and/or a pair of old dungarees.

His name was Bruce
    and/or Brett
    and/or Rick
I was single and looking for a soulmate.

He   *was/wasn't* married. I didn't care
to be a mistress. He visits our bijou Hackney bedsit on Mondays
    and/or we've had a cottage in Melksham for thirty years;
three kids, grandkids and an elderly Labrador
who traipses behind on our walks.

No more *Roxy*
    and/or Mirabelle
    and/or Teen-Dreamy
I'm no longer romantic, at least
that's what my badge says.

Waiting for Bread

We press lips to cold glass
to see if they stick.

It's a risk— but they don't.
I admire our lip-marks

and giggle as she says
I know a way of warming up.

Our snoggy cloud-breath
rises with the morning.

At last, a rattle of keys.
The door opens

to that hot, yeasty aroma
pulling us in.

My fifteen-year-old hymen

was pricked by a Welsh vicar's son.
Casually refusing a condom, he declared,
It's like having a bath with your socks on.

In shared bedsit gloom, two other lads slept on.
Heavy with sock-whiff, the room averted its eyes
when our heavy petting breached its code.

No fireworks, just a sly squib slipped in.
A friend's mum who worked in Family Planning
got me a test. Followed by homebrew – *cheers!*

Later I learned that Gethin was a virgin,
who'd never had a bath with socks on
and we both turned out queer.

Proposal

Given the chance, we'd have swapped his pants
for my dresses. The boy next door played
with my doll's house. Bedsits in the pear tree,
string and tin-can telephone, tricycle races
to the woodshed, yelling: *See you in Africa.*

The day his mother caught us, pants down,
round the side of our house, I nearly ran
from home. When he was four, me seven,
he popped the question, puzzled over
how to marry Greek Orthodox with Jew.

He trained at Claridges, inherited his parents'
country hotel, survived AIDS for eight years.
At the funeral, I told that story.
It was the only proposal he ever made.
All the guys in leather wept into lace.

Diva

Lipstick mouth, sex-pot pout. She plucks
her vocal strings pizzicato. Her Quattro Stagioni
hair tosses rain-glitter under streetlight.
Her audience – night's echo. Her voice adagios
through winter, glissandos into spring. She summer-dives
with swifts, makes careful footprints in snow.
She scoops sweetness into the blossom purse that she
presses beneath her ribs, between her thighs.

Ronnie Scott's 1976

Some nights, I'd wade through
crowds, loaded tray on one arm, the other
shielding bumps. Trios and quintets oozed
syncopated scats and Bebop, while *Roxy Beaujolais,*
the Australian barmaid, sat reading Proust with her feet
in an ice bucket. Norwegians straight off the rigs
drank pints and shorts by the score.

Portuguese Roy the maître d was a fixer; he fixed me
to be dresser to Earl Hines' singer when her
dreads caught in her zip, so I fixed her with
shopping trips and tarot readings. Earl *Fatha* Hines in his
horsehair wig, held backstage court to a nightly parade of musos
paying respect. Pete King sat counting takings: *Earl'll look after you,*
he said, but Earl was a mean dude, just a twenty
for a week of chasing my arse. A pound a night plus tips
was the deal; the graveyard section meant lousy sightlines
and no pay. At two a.m. Ronnie draped round a pillar for his
traditional farewell … *an' if we don't see you next month, have a nice life.*
Then we'd spill into Soho looking for action or a cab.

Clint played with Stan Getz when his double-bass fingers
plucked my strings. I fell for his Afro, his velvet voice, but
he left me with crabs. George Melly who couldn't be trusted
with the dressing-room key, tried to invite me home with his
wife and boyfriend. Always that thrill as I stepped through the door.
Everyone left their lives with the hatcheck girl for the table-lamp
smoky dark, for Blossom Deary's whine, Dizzie's inflatable cheeks
and Tom Waits' gravel tones Singing: *The piano's bin drinkin'.*
Soho was safe, because within hours of joining the staff,
the Maltese gangs, the strip-joint owners knew exactly
who I was and where I belonged.

Susan Expects to Be Admired

Susan is eternally blessed with clean hands. Her glands
discreet, as is her depression. Her nails fortified,
forbidden to split. Her middle name is Elizabeth
or Catherine, but never Liz or Kate.

Her squeaky blonde hair minds its manners.
Her mouth retains a pleasant up-turn
when making catty remarks to classmate Jane,
Thelma's such a lump, hasn't even got the proper shoes.

Susan's mother sends her to ballet class
so her posture and grace will captivate
the right kind of boy. Her designer wardrobe
will be funded by business expenses.

Susan is popular, but careful not to stand out. She plans
for two babies, one of each, and a semi-
detached in Bibby Road. They will spend Sundays
swimming in a private pool at the club.

What she doesn't plan for, is her daughter
joining the 5th Regiment Royal Artillery –
or for her son to take amphetamines
and run off with the lad from the chippie.

Dateroo

He's her buy-one-get-one-free.
She's his twitter-pie, his premier league.

Tucking into each other like two-for-one at Wetherspoons,
they nod the same wink, sing from the same playlist. He grins
at her pissed totter, she caresses his tatts.

He's her fitbit, her chocky cupcake.
She's his favourite app, his tinny.

They are now an *us*, recruiting
mates to admire their attempts
to glue their faces together.

He's her Tinder Platinum prize.
She's his current swipe-right babe.

Araldite is murder to unstick after she goes viral.
She scrolls down his *My Top Pubes* collection and
spots a close-up of her Brazilian with bird tatt.

A Man Threw Knives at Me

When the man at the bar said
his assistant hadn't turned up
I thought, I know your game
but my mouth was reckless
and the words *I'll do it*
sprang from my lips.
I told him I was an actor
and could act scared.
I stood in front of the target.
He was blindfolded.
I was covered in paper
and heard the thud
of each knife
as it hit the board.
I kept repeating
this scenario.
The trouble was
I hadn't learned to tell
if the knife-throwers
always meant to aim
for the board.

Girl Golem is Stranded in Marriage

She sifts herself
through its dunes.
Its constant drift
lacks a fixed horizon.
Sand blasts any sense
of ceiling walls or self.
After eighteen months
without a compass
not even a mirage
of an oasis
can save her.

Removing Her Face

Woman at her mirror reaches for
a pink pot of remover-pads, wipes herself
away. Witch Hazel to finish the job.
Smothered in Lancôme lotion,
she smooths back to mummy
in a onesie.

Next day, she re-applies Revlon skin,
Maybelline eyes, lips, and pat of Yardley
against shine. With coral-pink smile
and cloud of Elnett hair, she heads
for the door. *Ready, darling.*
Am I OK?

Later, Maybelline-lips smile as she
steps back through the Witch Hazel door,
She re-applies mummy in a onesie.
Smooths back. The pot of pads
smears pink woman
from her mirror.

Full Sail

She feels like a ship in a bottle,
sails pulled erect, through its exit,
by a man with a string. He sighs
as he seals the bottle's neck.

He places her on an ornate shelf, where he
can keep an eye on her graceful lines.
She dreams of catching an evening tide
or finding a small but effective hammer.

Indoor Sport

He drags her round London
on a bicycle; pedal-crazy, panting
to catch up. She braves Hyde Park
Corner – stomach clenched.

Watch anything you like, he says.
Except when it's sport. Snooker,
rugby, tennis, darts and athletes
triumph to his cheers.

It's his indoor sport she dreads
when he empties his eyes, sharpens
his hand skills. Swift upper cut, slap, grab –
his trophies scrawled across her face.

Take the Medicine

It's no use hiding
in the pocket
of your vagina
his hand will
reach in will
hook line and
sink you then
will reel you in
make you take
the medicine
for his own good
swallow it down
now all of it open
your mouth show
your tongue swall-
ow the medicine

now take it

take it

Her Mind is Snagged

She keeps thinking about holes
in walls where a
        telephone or
        a painting
        no longer hung

She keeps thinking about a naked man
whose sink-hole eyes
could swallow a bus
Each room shuddered
        as he punished
        every surface of her
        possessions

She keeps thinking about a naked man
kneeling on her chest
forcing her to look as he
        pissed on her
        and her eyes
        were sucked into his

She keeps thinking about testicles
one three times bigger
and a private hospital room
where pain
        gripped him
        as he held her
        by the throat

Girl Golem Wonders What to Wear

Her golem body is obliged to
step into stockings, strap on a skirt that exposes
the tender gash between her legs.

She longs for trees and dungarees,
struggles to cross ankles, tuck them

to the side, knees together. Hands folded.
She feels as welcome as a hornet at a hen party.

Aged five, behind the garden shed,
she tries to scoop out a pear penis to wear,

attempts to stick it onto her tiny bud.
Like the rest of her, it doesn't fit.

When men whistle, she dons a monkey-grin.
In bed, she utters moans in all the right places.

She decides she is better off solo, cannot
imagine herself wheeling a gay-golem baby.

My Life as a Soap

Y'aright Luv is the title. The opening shot pans red-brick terraced houses while the brass band theme fades and I utter my opening line, *Well, I'll go to our scullery, Mum. Smell that germicide on me 'ands,* I say to the woman apparently playing my mother. *Yer daft 'apeth,* she replies. Gracie Fields shrieks *Sally, Sally, pride of our alley,* from the wireless on the sideboard. Our living room is a brightly lit studio set, its painted flats end in darkness. Steam pours out as Mum opens the oven. *Dinner's ready, lay t'table lass.* Suddenly the director yells, *CUT! Continuity please!*

We are surrounded by make-up artists, who shove a dark wig on my mother's head, wipe her face with remover that smells of lard. She's told to play her character older with a Jewish voice and I am given a false nose to wear. Roast pork is replaced by a big pot of chicken soup. The title has changed to *Oy Vey Luv?* and my new line is, *Vot can I do Mama?* The radio switches to klezmer melodies. I strive to turn every remark into a question, to shrug and use my hands more. Mother now clutches her chest with a gasp, whenever a catastrophe is mentioned on the news.

I ask the director how to play the part, when I'm also supposed to be a closet lesbian with a crush on her teacher. I find myself lingering over the thought of her face. *Stick to the script,* he says. *Inner tension is good for your character. Work it out.*

Puzzled

I used to slot into place
with a satisfying click

      Now my colours won't match
      and I've lost my edges

                  I struggle to
                  piece myself back together

stare at strewn fragments
unable to find any that interlock

My head is no longer

                the one in the box

     Once I was a thatched cottage,

          roses round its door

                Now I'm a lost island
                without palm trees or   beach

        I can no longer tell   sea   from sky
my horizon –
       just grey   mizzle

Out of My Head

Last year I slipped into His,
with its sour wine stink, mouldy heel
of bread in the fridge, fag-burns
on the sofa and razor-studded door.
Now I am homeless.

Hers seems a better option,
with its complementary colour scheme,
capacious bed, cosy curtains. Can I stay?
She'll hardly know I'm here.

And Eat It

I've nothing against éclairs,
their shape and choux,
chocolate slick on the outside,
and hidden cache of cream
waiting to burst. I relished them, but
secretly longed to concoct my own.

It was vanilla slices that did for me:
all pink and secret layers,
you can push the tip of your
tongue into. Lick the custard cream,
followed by a fairy cake with a cherry
to slip between your lips.

I Sketch Her as a Bird-headed Goddess

With stroke of pen, rub of charcoal, I capture
the spread of her arms, raised in blessing.

Her sideways stare examines me
like a specimen dung beetle.

The diagonal of her eyebrow accuses.
Our fixity of focus holds the gap

between us, the flutter and scratch
of my hand, the arrow of her glance.

I'm a queer bird, she says,
cocking her head. Her words

beak me like millet grain,
a worm to be considered.

La Cuisine de L'Amour

i.m. Gertrude Stein and Alice B. Toklas

Alice wore her blue gown and slight moustache. Wherever Gertrude
went, Alice was sure to go. Their love was a chalice, their home a palace,
or at least their *petit château*. Alice prepared:

plat de cabanon royal à la portmanteau

~§~

pintade à la crème de truffes

~§~

chemise en cocotte

Whatever Alice made, Gertrude ate her little pussy-wujum-pujum's
offerings and fed bread and fish to *Basket*, despite the rule. *Basket* was a
poodle, a noodle-doodle, *Aunty* was an ambulance that Gertrude drove,
delivering medical supplies, fetching wounded from the front at Ypres.
She said: *There is love between someone who is someone and another someone
who is everything.*

Always *le déjeuner sublime,*
rich enough for a genius, a them and us,
endless *soirées* with all the best *artistes.*

~§~

*PicassoCézanneMatisseDaliBraqueApollinaire
et l'oncle Tomme de Cobblie et tous.*

Alice was

~§~

her key holder,
her *crème de vache,*
her dance card,
her deal-breaker,
her typist *très rapide,*
son éditeur-en-chef,
son coup de poitrine,
son fait accompli.

Unfitting

After Caroline Bird

Like a glove on the wrong hand,
the moon out at noon. I was salt in tea,
shoving my leg into a sleeve,
stuck on the singles table at weddings,
stifling the crush on my best friend,
calling my partner *they*, or trying
to book a double room in a B&B.

How I distanced myself from those women
in the bar on the Kings Road,
where some wore cufflinks, others,
heavy perfume, tight dresses.
I couldn't bear a skirt, without
the safety of a gusset.

The chips from my shoulders make
a magnificent outfit: gloved, salty
and glued with gold.

Birls and Goys Come Out to Play

Oyez, Oyez, Oyez…

Come out, come out, wherever you are,
the moon is bright, the door's ajar.
It's time you came and you know how.
Dark as Guinness, bright as daisies

wicked as knickerbocker glories
with a cherry to pop.
Innocent as vegan smoothies
with a hint of Clapham sauce.

On with your mask
off with your mask
off to the hairdresser
up Queen Street
up Queers United
down the Butch Biker for a pint
down the bucket and spade beach
the one with twirly windmills.
Is your tide in? Is it out?

Get yer kecks off, yer PJs on
frock-up or dress down
glad rags or handbags
tache or jockstrap

DMs or lippie– just come.
Spectrums welcome.
Are you nearly there yet?
We'll wait – don't fret

come early, come late
as long as you can still come.

Goys: Yiddish for non-Jews

Power Cut

I was safe with   you on the
other side of   the world
the sight   and sound
of you   disturbs
tectonic   plates.
I know you're there
but you   can't see me
I found   your friend request
your page how you've aged
and now you're too close
like that   time you hunted
me down   your voice-
mail shook   me like those
other times   you punched my
thoughts out   even after
thirty years   they flicker
as I press   delete

Girl Golem Looks Back

So, G★d
Now I'm the *pisher,* the *alte cacker*
I managed your three score and ten –
so *nu?* What now?
Unfriend me?
Unspell me?
Undress me?
Unsex me?
Undo me?
Unhinge me?
Unknow me?
Unmake me?
Unme?
unm
תֱּמֱא

Pisher: pisser; *alte cacker*: old shitter; *nu*: what?: an interjection; תֱּמֱא: truth.

Tripp Reviews My Past

I would not go there again. Unborn babies. Needy children in closets, screaming *me, me, me*. All those hearts on the floor, you could sweep them up. Scalding scummy water and a pool you wouldn't risk shoving your ex into. The view of ☹ bins was not the sunlit cove in the ad. I wouldn't give it even 1★ let alone 3 ★★★. The only way to get back there is through the eye of a camel, that's rich! The host is a hookworm, whose rooms are tight as egg cells. Paper-thin walls give free-range access to next door's shenanigans and eternal extractor fan – so forget sleep. The corridors are piled with dirty-linen corpses. The timed light turns off before you've reached your room on the aspiration floor. And the food...

Dear Unborns

The first time –
　　　　pinned against
　　　　tree roots
　　　　he shoved into me
claimed my price for
a cheap Bolognese.
　　　　I uttered
the women's plea
to St. Rita –
Getitoverquick.

Eyes fixed
　　　　on branches.
　　　　Lights flicker
　　　　on leaves.
　　　　I knew
just feet from
the roar of traffic
you'd been planted.

The next time –
　　　　I was wedlocked
　　　　in a war
　　　　of attrition.
Only months after
his chemotherapy
　　　　I decided to leave
　　　　then you
　　　　entered my womb.

I just couldn't
　　　　I'm sorry. I
　　　　flushed you both out
　　　　before your hand
grew fingers.

A friend said
　　　　Some souls elect
　　　　this brevity.
Tell me, was she right?

Be Grateful For Those Love Lessons

1. First Love
You laid your body on the director's bed
and he taught you how lips and fingers lie.
You thought you were his leading lady,
until the night he entered, your best friend
on his arm. And you, the understudy.

2. The Husband
You fell for hippie cool, a beard grown long
in India, Iran, Afghanistan. You learned
to cook fallen market veg, to dry yourself
without a towel and if there's no paper,
to wipe your bum with a stone.

He taught you the sound of slap
and the quicksand of appeasement.
You learned how rage empties eyes,
digs chunks from walls, leaves homes
and hearts a splintered mess, and
that cancer is no excuse. You learned
that leaving didn't kill him after all.

3. The Girlfriend
She taught you to peg out washing tight—
no more ironing. You learned madness from her
laundry basket hurled downstairs, from her
door slammed shut for days. You learned
how words hit deepest, twisting you into
the crazy one. How incest infects the mind
of anyone too close to its survivor.

You fled, whooping all the way
to the shopping centre, but an
umbilical fear you could not grasp, or name,
dragged you back. When you pretended
you'd been for fags, she laughed
in your face, pegged the laundry tighter.

Tending the Wounded

1.
I made myself into a bandage
wrapped myself around him.
He was a jagged wound
who didn't know how to close.

I released the poison, had bruises
to prove it. I surgically removed
myself along with the foetus
that grew inside, like his tumour.

2.
I was a poultice and lay
myself over her.
She seeped into me,
turned my mind yellow.

I sectioned myself from her
and was a locked ward
until I learned how to fold
myself into my own arms.

Liberating the Senses

Has the elastic gone in your genitals?
Have you lost your twang?
When a sneeze holds more thrill,
why not reach for a good book and stroke
the sleek body of a cat wrapped round your leg?
Liberate yourself from urges that
only lead to kitchen-sink dramas.

Outside, an ash tree dangles leaves,
tosses them in wind. Cloud shadow shifts
across hills, meadows ripple
and somewhere, younger bodies
sweat, pump juices; lost to ecstasy.
Others insist, *you can never say never* –
but my lips are firmly sealed.

Seen

My winter face stares back,
dares meto meet its decline.
I survey my map of mishaps,
try to recall when I was last held.

I look at a photo of me aged twenty:
her smoulder-eyed beauty,
her blank-page face;
waiting for its story.

Mind riddled with gaps,
and gob full of opinions,
this body still stands, bends
and carries despite subsidence.

At my retina scan today, I saw the backs
of my eyes like unlaid eggs, an eye-tree
of scarlet tracery. The scan man said,
You still have fabulous retinas.

Because of Wet Grass

people whispered   into
mobiles
covered me
     with blankets   Skidding onto
my back
     something cracked
         someone
         with my voice
           screamed   *FUUCCK!*

After the repairs   the pain
neighbours
         friends   fetched me back
        to bipedal health
           but something   cracked me
     open   softer

     Seeing my   foot flap
           fractured   more
   than my ankle

   if I'm not my body
     then who?

What I Asked of Life

When I was six, Life gave me cartwheels, bilberry pie
and all of us at the mirror, comparing purpled tongues.

From thirteen to thirty I pleaded, *Give me a Christian nose,*
legs up to my armpits. And please, stop me having crushes on girls.

But I stayed a long-nosed Jew, too smart to get a boyfriend,
too scared to get a girlfriend. *Not listening!* said Life, *Deal with it.*

Come, said Life, holding out her little finger, *let's make friends.*
So we shook pinkies and my mishmash-self grew potato-smooth.

Rewilding the Body

Based on Isobella Tree's account of rewilding Knepp Farm

Let thistle stitch my wounds,
as painted-lady caterpillars feast
on the prickles.

Let pigs unzip my paths,
with cracks for bastard toadflax
and meadow-clary.

Let ragwort flourish
as one hundred and seventy-seven
insect species thrive on its bad reputation.

Let longhorn cattle tramp
hoof-print pools for fairy shrimp,
water crowfoot, stonewort.

And one moonlit night – nightingales
will return to fill my country
with their song.

Sometime in the next ten years

your paintings will go to the tip, your clothes
in bin-bags will fetch forty-three pence per kilo
at unit six on the trading estate. Someone
will replace the patio, convert the workshop
to kitchen-diner and rip out the bathroom.

Like you, they might stand in the garden
and plan how to redesign the planting.
Perhaps they too will gaze at the distant hills
muttering, *They'll carry me out in a box*.

When your body has run its last errand,
when its burden of flesh becomes light
as snow or ash, it sends flurries into dusk.
Do not mistake your last golden hour
of flame for a new dawn. Witness the burn.
Give thanks. Leave it to curl on the wind.

You'll never be anyone else

so you – yes you, with your warts and wings
will just have to do.

Acceptance is your food and shelter, without which
you are brushwood

left to the mercy of any foul wind.
Stop drinking the poison

labelled *Hate me*. It's that simple.
I didn't say easy.

Acknowledgements

My heartfelt thanks go to Caleb Parkin, Carrie Etter, Jinny Fisher, Julia Webb, Ama Bolton, Michelle Diaz, Morag Kiziewicz and Jessica Mookherjee, for their essential and enduring support.

Versions of some of the poems have appeared in the following journals: *Domestic Cherry, The Rialto, Tears in the Fence, Under the Radar, Prole, Rat's Ass, Poetry Space, Obsessed with Pipework, Shearsman, Lighthouse, Riggwelter, Ink Sweat and Tears, London Grip,* and *Poetry Wales*.

Other poems appeared in the anthologies: *#Me Too, A Women's Poetry Anthology* edited by Deborah Alma, *The Book of Love and Loss: Poems for Today* edited by R.V. Bailey and June Hall, and, *Queer Writing for a Brave New World* edited by Out on the Page.